REGGIE WHITE

Star Defensive Lineman

BY BILL GUTMAN

MILLBROOK SPORTS WORLD

THE MILLBROOK PRESS

BROOKFIELD, CONNECTICUT

Photographs courtesy of: Allsport USA: cover, pp. 3 (Jonathan Daniel), 24–25 (Stephen Dunn), 42 (Jonathan Daniel), 45 (Earl Richardson); Green Bay Packers: cover inset; *Sports Illustrated:* pp. 4 (Anthony Neste), 37 (John Biever), 40 (Bill Ballenberg); Vern Biever: pp. 7, 33; *Chattanooga Times:* p. 11; University of Tennessee Sports Department: pp. 12, 16–17, 18; NFL Photos: pp. 21 (Paul Spinelli), 26 (NFL Alumni); AP/Wide World: pp. 22, 28, 31, 34–35; Ed Mahan: p. 29; *Philadelphia Inquirer:* p. 38.

Library of Congress Cataloging-in-Publication Data
Gutman, Bill.
Reggie White : star defensive lineman / by Bill Gutman.
p. cm.— (Millbrook sports world)
Includes bibliographical references and index.
Summary: The story of the all-pro defensive end Reggie White.
ISBN 1-56294-461-4
1. White, Reggie—Juvenile literature. 2. Football players—
United States—Biography—Juvenile literature. [1. White,
Reggie. 2. Football players. 3. Afro-Americans—Biography.]
I. Title. II. Series.
GV939.W43G88 1994
796.332'092— dc20 [B] 93-38960 CIP AC

Published by The Millbrook Press
2 Old New Milford Road
Brookfield, Connecticut 06804

REGGIE WHITE

Every time Reggie White gets down on the line of scrimmage, he knows his opponents will try everything to stop him. A game against the New York Giants on October 8, 1989, was a perfect example. The Philadelphia Eagles' all-pro defensive end found himself facing two Giants blockers on nearly every play. They were 275-pound (125-kilogram) tackle Doug Riesenberg and 245-pound (111-kilogram) tight end Mark Bavaro. Their job was to keep the 285-pound (129-kilogram) Reggie from reaching New York quarterback Phil Simms and from stopping the New York ball carriers.

It took Reggie just four plays on that day to show why he was such a great football player. He came to the line and saw that the Giants had three tight ends lined up on the same side of the field.

"I knew a run was coming my way," he said later.

At the snap, quarterback Simms turned and gave the ball to running back O. J. Anderson, who began moving toward Reggie's side of the line.

Doing what he does best, Reggie White sacks New York Giants quarterback Phil Simms for a loss. At the end of the 1992 season Reggie was the only player in NFL history to have more quarterback sacks than games played.

Sure enough, both Riesenberg and Bavaro went right at Reggie. They were hoping to hit him hard at the same time and take him out of the play. If they did, Anderson would have a good chance to get through the hole and run for a sizable gain.

But Reggie White had other ideas. "In high school and college you're taught to hit the ground on a double team," he said. "In the NFL you're supposed to take it on. I get double-teamed on every play, so I expect it."

Once he saw Anderson with the ball, Reggie decided to use his great power. He stayed high and fought off the double block with what is called a "rip," a hard uppercut move with his right arm. It was such a strong move that it split Riesenberg and Bavaro enough for Reggie to slice through and tackle Anderson after just a 2-yard gain.

The next time the Giants had the ball, Reggie switched from power to speed. This time he just burst past the startled Riesenberg. He used a right-arm rip and then a shoulder slap with his left hand to get by Bavaro. Then he ran wide, leaning to the inside, and reached out to tackle quarterback Simms before he could throw the ball.

It was yet another quarterback sack for the only player in NFL history to have more sacks than games played. In fact, many are now calling Reggie the best defensive lineman ever.

But there's more to Reggie White than sheer strength and speed. He plays a position where there are bone-shattering collisions on every play, yet Reggie is a gentle, loving man. He is, in fact, an ordained minister whose primary goal in life is to help people and spread the word of God.

"People have to realize that football is aggressive, not violent," Reggie has said. "Violence is what's happening on our streets, where kids are dying. Football is a very aggressive game . . . but we're not killing each other. I'm going to play hard, but I won't ever go out on the field with the idea of hurting somebody.''

And unlike many of today's superstars, Reggie White will quickly admit that he *is* a role model for youngsters. It's a responsibility he takes very seriously.

''I don't think a lot of athletes really want to be [role models],'' he has said. ''But whether we choose [to be] or not, we are in the public's eye. People are going to be looking at us. We've got kids and adults who make us their heroes, and that gives us a responsibility.''

Signing autographs for kids is, for Reggie, a satisfying part of his job.

Reggie also takes football very seriously. Playing a position where there is a high rate of injury, he started 120 straight games through the end of the 1992 season. There is little doubt that the way he has played will someday result in his being voted into the Pro Football Hall of Fame.

A BIG KID WITH TALENT

Reggie White is a prime example of a person who came from humble beginnings to become an outstanding citizen. But unlike some others, Reggie has never forgotten his roots. He was born in Chattanooga, Tennessee, on December 19, 1961. His parents split up when he was very young, and his early years were not easy ones.

The family didn't have much money back then, and sometimes Reggie had to stay with his grandmother, who lived in the inner city of Chattanooga. He found that living in the projects was very difficult. By the time he was nine years old he was learning how to fight.

"I grew up a fighter then," Reggie recalled. "One year in the projects was tough, even then. It might not be as tough as it is today, but it was tough."

His mother, Thelma, eventually remarried. Reggie accepted his new stepfather, Leonard Collier, and turned the change in his life into a positive thing.

"When my mother married my stepdad we got along real well as a family. That's what I mean when I say that role models start at home."

It wasn't always as easy with his real father. Charlie White was not only a great athlete, but also a leader in the civil rights movement in

Chattanooga. He and his brother, Reggie's uncle Al, were both outstanding softball players and the first black men to integrate the city league in the 1960s. Yet there was a time when father and son saw very little of each other. It took many years before those wounds healed. Today, however, they are very close.

Sam Woolwine, a sportswriter with the *Chattanooga News-Free Press,* isn't surprised by Reggie's athletic success. He says there were great athletes on both sides of the family.

"Reggie came from a very athletic background," Woolwine explained. "His uncle, Al, once hit a softball clean out of the Gator Bowl in Jacksonville, Florida. And his grandfather on his mother's side, Clarence Dodd, was supposed to be an unbelievable athlete."

Reggie grew very quickly. He was always bigger than most other kids his age. But that didn't mean they never teased him.

"Kids used to call me names like 'Bigfoot' and 'Land of the Giant,' " he said. "Then they would run away. When I was in the seventh grade I found something I was good at. I could play football. I could use my size and achieve success by playing within the rules."

Although Reggie always loved football the most, he soon became a fine all-around athlete. He played baseball and was also an outstanding basketball player. But he seemed to know early on that football would be his ticket to success. He gave up baseball when he finished the Dixie Youth League at about the age of 12. He played basketball through high school.

"I remember telling my mother that someday I would be a professional football player and I'd take care of her for the rest of her life," Reggie explained.

But there was always something else in his life as well.

"When I was about ten years old I felt inside that God was calling me to something great," he said. "I didn't know what and I didn't know how. But I just felt it."

By the time he was 12, Reggie was telling his mother he would be not only a pro football player but a minister as well. As a young teen, Reggie idolized a minister, the Reverend Paul Ferguson. This man had a great influence on young Reggie. What made the relationship unusual was that Paul Ferguson was white.

"He was a white minister in an all-black church," said Reggie. "Reverend Ferguson was the greatest man of God I ever saw. He had a way with kids and with teaching. I always wanted to be a Christian, but I never knew how. He said that understanding was the first thing I had to know."

Reggie continued to study and learn about God. At the age of 17, he became an ordained Baptist minister. His faith would become stronger with each passing year.

So did his football talent. The more Reggie played, the better he got. He was bigger and stronger each year, and by the time he reached Howard High School in Chattanooga he looked like a real star. In the fall of 1977 the Howard Tigers had a real tiger by the tail.

As good as Reggie was, Howard never really had much of a team. Reggie was a fine offensive lineman and a real anchor at defensive tackle. But the first two years the team couldn't even get over the .500 mark. It was a different story with the basketball team. By his junior year, the 6-foot-4-inch (193-centimeter) Reggie started at center and helped lead Coach Henry Bowles' club into the finals of the state tournament.

When he returned for his senior year in the fall of 1979, Reggie weighed nearly 240 pounds (109 kilograms) and was almost at his full height of 6 feet 5 inches (195 centimeters). This time he took the gridiron by storm. Reggie was a terror all year. He was the team leader with his fierce line play and helped take the Tigers to a winning season.

Howard won three straight games at one point and also defeated its arch rival, the McCallie School. The team didn't win a championship, but finished at 6–4 for its best record since 1971. Without a title, the highlight of the season had to be the play of Reggie White.

He was not only an all-state defensive tackle, but a consensus high school All-American as well. Defensively, he had 88 solo tackles, 52 assists, and 10 sacks. In addition, he was rated the number one collegiate prospect in the state of Tennessee. But that wasn't all.

Reggie followed with another outstanding basketball season, helping the Howard Tigers to the state finals once again. This time he made the All-State

At 6 feet 4 inches (193 centimeters) tall, Reggie was an outstanding center on the Howard High basketball team.

and All-Tournament teams as a center. *The Chattanooga Times* named him Player of the Year in both football and basketball, the only player ever to receive both of those honors in the same year.

Reggie was a good student as well as a top athlete. The question was never *if* he would go to college—it was *where* he would go to college.

OFF TO TENNESSEE

Like most star high school athletes, Reggie had his choice of many top colleges. But when it came down to a decision, Reggie said he wanted to stay close to his roots and to his family. He accepted an offer to attend the University of Tennessee.

Coach Johnny Majors was trying to rebuild the Tennessee program. He wanted to make the Volunteers one of the top teams in the country. He hoped the big, strong, fast kid from Howard High would help anchor the team for the next four years.

On the field, Reggie seemed right on schedule. He became the first freshman in 1980 to win a starting position, moving in at defensive tackle early in the season. In just his second start, he was the team's defensive player of the week. There was little doubt that he had super talent.

The Volunteers, however, were not a very good team in 1980. They finished the season with a disappointing 5–6 record. Reggie made his

It didn't take Reggie long to become a star at the University of Tennessee. This official publicity shot shows the power, size, and speed that made Reggie great.

mark with 32 tackles, 19 assists, a pair of fumble recoveries, and 2 sacks of opposing quarterbacks.

"My first goal was to do well enough to become a starter, and now I have," he said. "I'm comfortable with my season. But [the team's] season has been a letdown. I thought with our schedule we'd win a few big games and be on our way."

But the disappointment only made Reggie work harder. A year later he was back and better than ever. This time he put together a great season, and pro scouts were already rating him as a top NFL prospect. He finished his sophomore year with 61 tackles, 34 assists, and 8 quarterback sacks.

He also enjoyed the season because now the Volunteers were a winning team. They finished at 8–4, including a 28–21 win over Wisconsin in the Garden State Bowl. Reggie then was named to the defensive line on the *Football News'* Sophomore All-American team.

The Tennessee coaches credited him with 22 "big plays" in 1981, 11 more than anyone else on the team. He tackled ball carriers seven times for losses, and at one point blocked extra points in three straight games. It takes both power and speed to do that.

"Reggie could become one of the finest defensive linemen I've ever coached," said Johnny Majors. "Some of the things he did this past year were amazing. He made some plays ordinary football players couldn't make. He has natural talent and also great depth of character."

No one ever questioned Reggie White's character. He continued to make good grades in his classes and continued his work as an ordained minister. But just when everyone was expecting a big All-American season in 1982, Reggie White was tested as never before.

THE ROAD TO SUPERSTARDOM

When Reggie returned for spring practice in March of 1982, the coaches' eyes popped. He now weighed a solid 270 pounds (122 kilograms). Yet he was as fast as ever. He ran a 40-yard (37-meter) dash in 4.7 seconds. That's a lot of speed for a man his size. He was also one of only five Tennessee players who could bench-press more than 400 pounds (180 kilograms). Everyone said that 1982 would be an All-American season for him. But on a football field, things can change in a hurry.

This time injuries were the problem. Reggie was hurt from the season's start. It seemed as if he had one injury after another. It was not easy to overcome two sprained ankles, a pinched nerve in his neck, and a chipped bone in his elbow. They were all injuries that slowed him down. In fact, he finally needed surgery on his injured elbow.

Needless to say, Reggie did not produce an All-American year. His numbers were down. He had just 36 tackles and 11 assists. But he still managed seven quarterback sacks. Yet with the team slipping back to 6–5–1, the season was a big disappointment for everyone.

"It certainly wasn't the kind of year I had hoped for," Reggie said. "I had never been injured in my whole time playing football. Even though I tried to give everything I had, I just couldn't do it."

When his senior year of 1983 came, Reggie White felt he had something to prove. He worked hard again during the off-season because he felt there was a lot at stake.

"This season could mean a pro football career for me," he said. "That would help my family the way I want to and help me to start a ministry. So I'm not holding back."

Once the season started, Reggie White began to play as well as any defensive tackle in the land. He had a big game almost every week. In the season opener he outplayed Pittsburgh's All-American offensive tackle Bill Fralic. Shortly afterward, the Vols beat Louisiana State, 20–6. In that one, Reggie had five tackles and two assists, one sack, and two stops for lost yardage. He was named Southeastern Conference Lineman of the Week by both the Associated Press and United Press International.

By then, his teammates had nicknamed him the ''Minister of Defense,'' and soon after they voted him permanent team captain for 1983. That was a real honor. Still, Reggie wasn't letting up.

''I've worked to make this my best year ever and I'm not accepting anything less than the best,'' he said.

In a game against Georgia Tech, Reggie is about to put the clamps on the Yellow Jackets quarterback. During his years at Tennessee, Reggie was a master at sacking.

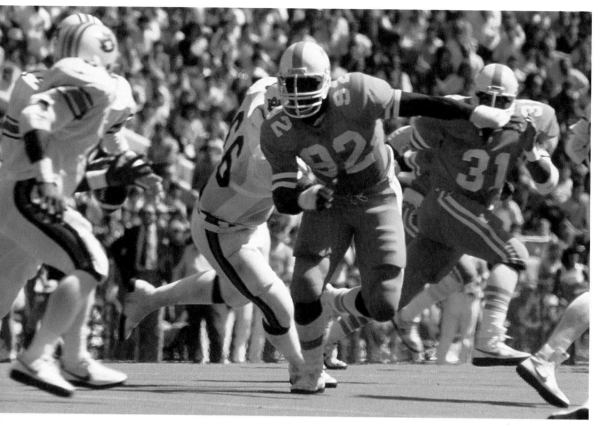

A consensus All-American as a Tennessee senior, Reggie had speed as well as power. Once he was past his blocker, Reggie (92) could often run down quarterbacks and speedy halfbacks.

For the first time since Reggie arrived in Knoxville, the Volunteers were a top 20 team. He continued to play hard, and Coach Majors had more praise for him.

"I've seen no one who could outplay him this year," the coach said. "He's playing like the best in the country at his position. Reggie is the most physically capable lineman I've ever had. He has size, strength, quickness, and speed. He just dominates a defense.''

But Reggie didn't take all the credit. With the entire Tennessee defense doing a fine job, the star tackle wanted the praise to be passed around.

''I couldn't be having this kind of year without getting the backup from the rest of the defense,'' he said. ''To do all these things I had to have help from the ten other guys on the field.''

There was now little doubt that a healthy Reggie White was a bona fide All-American. Even before the season ended, he became Tennessee's all-time sack leader.

Six times in 1983 the coaches named him Defensive Player of the Game. The Vols finished the regular season at 8–3, then met Maryland in the Florida Citrus Bowl in mid-December.

It would be Reggie's final game as collegian. He was great again as Tennessee upset Maryland, 30–23, to finish at 9–3. Reggie completed his senior year with 72 tackles, 28 assists, and a team-record 15 quarterback sacks. He also had a fumble recovery and a pass interception.

Needless to say, he was a consensus All-American and also chosen as Player of the Year in the Southeastern Conference. He was also one of the four finalists for the Lombardi Trophy, given annually to the nation's outstanding lineman. Many felt he should have won it.

But that didn't really matter. Reggie White had set out to prove something at the outset of his senior year. He wanted to be known as one of the best football linemen in the country. Now, he was. The next step was not hard to guess: It would be pro football.

A SURPRISE FIRST CHOICE

Reggie had always made good grades at Tennessee. He was a human services major, and getting his degree was very important to him. With his final football season over, it seemed just a matter of finishing his courses so he could graduate. Then he would turn pro.

But in 1984 there was a new professional football league that played its games in the spring. It was called the United States Football League (USFL). The USFL held its draft in December 1983 and hoped to get as many good players as it could.

Not surprisingly, Reggie White was a top choice. He was picked by the Memphis Showboats. Reggie knew that if he signed with the new league he would have to begin playing in January. That would mean dropping out of school. So he had to make a big decision.

Reggie was very close to getting his college degree. But the USFL was offering the kind of money that could really help his family. He decided to take the offer. But he also promised himself he would return to Tennessee to get his degree. (Several years later he did complete his B.A. in human services. Reggie wasn't the kind of person to leave anything undone.)

In mid-January 1984, he signed a five-year, $3.8 million contract with the Showboats. He would get a signing bonus and a yearly salary. In addition, the Showboats agreed that in the case of Reggie's death, his family would get money for the rest of their lives. That was the kind of insurance Reggie was looking for.

"I'm very happy right now," Reggie said. "I'm satisfied with the deal and I'm looking forward to Memphis. My family is also taking it well and they are very proud."

So the "Minister of Defense" was now a pro. He soon began playing outstanding football once again. Reggie started 16 games for the Showboats in 1984 and promptly made the USFL all-rookie team. He had 52 solo tackles and 11 sacks in his first pro season. He was a star, but in a league that had still not gained total respect.

In the spring of 1985 he was back with the Showboats. But there were already rumors that the USFL was running out of money. If the league folded, the older National Football League (NFL) would come after the best USFL players. And everyone knew Reggie was one of the best.

He had another great season. He started all 18 regular-season games and two more in the playoffs. When it was over, he was a first team All-USFL selection. He had 68 solo tackles and 12.5 sacks. That was third best in the league. His aggressive play forced five fumbles, and he also recovered one.

Reggie had become a USFL superstar. But by late summer of 1985 things looked very bad, and many USFL teams began selling the rights to their players to rival

Reggie surprised a lot of people in 1984 by joining the Memphis Showboats of the new United States Football League. He became a star at Memphis and stayed with the Showboats for two years until the USFL folded.

In the fall of 1985, Reggie (shown here with Eagles owner Norman Braman) signed with the Philadelphia Eagles. Reggie would later become an even bigger star in the National Football League.

NFL teams. On September 20, the Philadelphia Eagles purchased the rights to Reggie White. The Eagles had picked Reggie in a special NFL draft the year before.

Reggie thought about the change he would have to make. He talked it over with his wife, Sara. Finally they decided that Reggie would play in Philadelphia.

By the time Reggie signed a contract and got to practice with his new teammates, the NFL season had already started. To make things even harder, Reggie and the other USFL players had already played an 18-game spring schedule. Playing two football seasons in one year is not an easy thing for the body to take. The weekly bumps and bruises don't have a chance to heal.

But by the Eagles' fourth game, Reggie was ready. He was joining a Philadelphia team that was coming off three straight losing seasons. The team had lost two of its first three games and would now be facing one of its divisional rivals, the New York Giants. Reggie didn't start the game, but it wasn't long before he was in there.

He quickly showed that he belonged. Reggie played a truly great game. Twice he sacked Giants' quarterback Phil Simms by himself. Another time he was given half a sack as he and a teammate hit Simms at the same time. Later, he deflected a pass at the line of scrimmage. Defensive back Herman Edwards picked the ball off and returned it for a score. The only bad part was that the Eagles lost in overtime, 16–10.

A week later, however, Reggie became a starter, playing left defensive end on the Eagles' three-man front line. After that, the position was his. Before his first NFL season had ended, Reggie White had proved he was one of the best in any league.

After playing 18 games with the Showboats, Reggie played another 13 with the Eagles, starting the last 12. He finished with 62 tackles and 38 assists as well as 13 sacks—fifth best in the National Football Conference (NFC). When the season ended he was named NFC Defensive Rookie of the Year by the Players Association. He was also on the all-rookie team and was an honorable mention all-pro. Reggie was on his way.

ALL-PRO AND MORE

In 1986, Reggie White showed the entire National Football League the kind of player he was. The team had a new coach, Buddy Ryan, who loved to build a strong defense. He was Reggie's kind of coach. And while the Eagles would finish the season at 5–10–1, Reggie was already close to being number one at his position.

This time he had 83 unassisted tackles and 18 sacks in 16 games. He was third in sacks behind a couple of pretty big names. Linebacker Lawrence Taylor of the Giants had 20.5, while defensive end Dexter Manley of the Redskins had 18.5. In addition, Reggie was a first team All-NFL selection and first team All-NFC pick. So he was an all-pro his first full year in the league.

As soon as he joined the Eagles, Reggie was a force. Veteran offensive linemen found it impossible to stop this young defensive end. NFL quarterbacks quickly became used to seeing Number 92 swooping down on them.

He was also chosen as a starter in the Pro Bowl game and was named the game's Most Valuable Player when he tied a Pro Bowl record with four sacks. He had done all this at the age of 25.

A year later, in 1987, Reggie put together another remarkable season. There was a players' strike that year, and the regulars played only 12 games. But Reggie still had 21 quarterback sacks. That was one short of the league record. He had at least one sack in 11 of the 12 games, and had 9 games in which he had more than one sack.

Now he was recognized by everyone. Several polls named him NFL Defensive Player of the Year. He was a unanimous All-NFL first team pick, the Eagles' Most Valuable Player and a Pro Bowl starter once more. In a game against the Redskins, Reggie made an amazing play. He swooped in on Washington quarterback Doug Williams, stole the ball out of his hands, and ran 70 yards for an Eagles' touchdown. Even though he weighed 285 pounds (129 kilograms), no Washington player could catch him as he ran to the end zone.

The next year, 1988, the Eagles finished at 10–6 and won the NFC Eastern Division title. Although they lost to the Chicago Bears in the divisional playoffs, 20–12, the team had a great season. So did Reggie White. He led the league in sacks again, this time with 18, and was a named NFL Player of the Year by the Washington Touchdown Club. He was a unanimous Pro Bowl choice and led the Eagles with 133 big tackles, 96 of them solo stops. Many were now calling him one of the best of all time.

Reggie received the Defensive Lineman of the Year Award in 1987 from the NFL alumni. It was one of many prizes he would get during his great career.

Football isn't all bone-crunching collisions and banged-up bodies. The camaraderie among teammates is often what makes the game fun. One day Reggie surprised his Eagles teammates by arriving at practice dressed as Batman.

Even more amazing was the fact that Reggie was in there every week. He never missed a game. According to Reggie, a defensive lineman has to have a built-in survival instinct. Even though he plays in the so-called trenches with the collisions and pileups, he has to be aware of everything around him.

During one game in 1988, Reggie was blocked by the offensive tackle. At the same time, the fullback dove to the outside and whipped his legs toward Reggie's ankles. Seeing this, the offensive tackle tried to push Reggie into the fullback's legs and then over a pile of bodies. With a quick skip back, Reggie avoided the fullback's leg whip. Then he spun around and avoided being pushed onto the pile. He walked away from the play.

"This is something you have to do or you won't line up the next week," Reggie explained. "You don't say, 'Okay, now I'm going to pull my ankle away. Now I feel pressure from the back, so I'll spin.' It's all reaction. Sometimes I don't even know what I did until I look at the films."

Some of the blocking schemes used against Reggie could be brutal. While they were not intended to hurt him, a serious injury could happen easily. Sometimes Reggie has had to contend with the wipeout block. That's when an offensive lineman goes low and comes flying at the defensive lineman's knees. With his quickness, Reggie could usually pull away just in time.

"It's a vicious blocking scheme," he admitted. "It can wipe a guy's knee out, but you can't complain because it isn't illegal, not on a running play. All you can do is try to be aware of everything happening around you. Keep the searchlights going, we call it."

Reggie said he doesn't think about serious injury very often. "You don't say to yourself, 'Gee, that one could have ended my career,' " he explained.

Although he played hard and at a consistent all-pro level, he always stayed controlled on the field. No one ever heard him curse, and he just wouldn't fight on the field.

Reggie and good friend Randall Cunningham formed the heart and soul of the Eagles in the late 1980s. Cunningham led the offense with his often sensational play at quarterback. Reggie led a rough, tough, hard-hitting defense that was feared all around the league.

"Maybe a little pushing or shoving sometimes," he admitted, "but that's it."

That side of Reggie came from his Christian upbringing and unswerving faith in God. He lived by certain principles that were always the most important things in his life.

BECOMING A PACKER

During the late 1980s and into the 1990s, Reggie continued to play outstanding football. He was an all-pro every year and never missed a game. And he was still the only player in NFL history to have more sacks than games played. But one thing began to bother him more and more with each passing year.

In all his years in sports, none of the teams he played on had ever won a championship—not in high school, not in college, not in the pros. For a few years it looked as if the Eagles had a chance. But the team always fell short. That's what happened again in 1992.

"I'm more than hungry for a championship," he said. "I'm starving for one."

Reggie went out and had another outstanding year. As usual, he started every game. He was involved in 81 tackles and added 14 more sacks to his growing ledger. That gave him 124 sacks in 121 NFL games.

A player like Reggie never quits on a play until the whistle blows. In this photo of a game against the Cardinals, Reggie is seen using his strength and quickness to recover a Phoenix fumble at the goal line.

He even scored a touchdown when he ran 37 yards with a fumble recovery at Phoenix on September 13.

The Eagles made the playoffs with an 11–5 record under new coach Rich Kotite, and then defeated New Orleans in the first round, 36–20. But in the next round they were beaten by the Dallas Cowboys, 34–10. The Cowboys went on to win the Super Bowl, and Reggie was disappointed again.

After the season, the NFL passed new rules that allowed many players to become free agents. That meant they could change teams on their own. Reggie was one of the players who could be a free agent. Though he loved playing in Philadelphia, Reggie began to think it was time for a change. Even though he was 31 years old, he felt he was still at the top of his game.

I don't think I've lost anything,'' he said. ''I wish I were a little lighter, but I feel like I'm a smarter player now.''

Teammates and opponents alike also said he was still among the best. Eagles' center David Alexander said that Reggie was ''in the best shape I've ever seen him.''

Reggie had also said he wanted to play for three or four more years. While he said that becoming the NFL's all-time sack leader would be an honor, it wasn't his ultimate goal.

''A championship means more to me than anything,'' he said.

Finally, Reggie made his decision. He would become a free agent and join a new team for 1993. When the other teams heard Reggie was available, they all wanted him. Teams began inviting him to their cities to try to win him over.

In April of 1993, Reggie became a free agent and left the Eagles to sign a four-year, $17-million deal with the Green Bay Packers. Reggie sits alongside Packers Coach Mike Holmgren (at left) at a press conference announcing his signing.

He spoke to coaches from many teams. He visited Cleveland, New York, Atlanta, Detroit, Green Bay, and Washington. Many felt he would sign with a strong team that had a real good chance to win the Super Bowl. But Reggie surprised everyone again. In early April it was announced that Reggie had signed a four-year contract with the Green Bay Packers. The deal was said to be worth about $17 million.

Reggie's choice surprised many because the Packers were not considered one of the best teams in the league. And Green Bay was not a big city, the kind of place Reggie seemed to prefer. But the Packers had had many great players over the years, and had a long-standing winning tradition. Now they were a young team that was getting better.

"People will say I went for the money," Reggie said, "and the money did have something to do with it. But the money gives me an opportunity to build businesses, create housing, and create opportunities for people in the inner city. I want to do that all over the country.

"I made the decision, and I'm happy to be a Packer."

As a Packer, Reggie was up to his old sacking tricks. Here he is about to lower the boom on Kansas City quarterback Dave Krieg.

GIVING BACK

Sam Woolwine of the *Chattanooga News-Free Press* remembers the first time he saw Reggie White. ''He had a Bible under one arm and a football under the other,'' Woolwine recalls. ''And you know he hasn't changed. I've seen a lot of shams and phonies, but Reggie isn't one of them. He has been very consistent in his life-style ever since his high school years.''

Reggie's belief in God has been long-standing and deep. Since becoming an ordained Baptist minister at 17, he has preached at more than 100 churches. He has also donated sizable amounts of money to several churches.

''Some players find this hard to understand,'' said Reggie. ''They ask me, 'Do you really have to do that?' I tell them yes, I have to give back to the Lord.''

He has also given in other ways. In recent years the plight of the inner cities has affected him deeply. In Philadelphia, Reggie and a few of his teammates visited the projects often, speaking to as many people as they could. Running back Keith Byars, who often went with Reggie, said the big, gentle man had a real effect on the people, especially youngsters.

''Kids see him but can't believe it's really him,'' Byars said. ''It's like, 'What are you doing down here?' It's an initial shock to these people. The kids reach out to him like he isn't real.''

Reggie White's popularity has turned
him into the pied piper of football
for young and old alike.

Reggie has said that more people must help kids living in the inner cities. ''Our government must take more action,'' he said. ''Many politicians don't understand what's happening in the inner city. People are struggling just to stay alive and that shouldn't be happening in this country.

Being out in the community has always been important to Reggie. He often walks the streets talking to fans. Here he speaks to a group of senior citizens at a Philadelphia housing project.

"I look at the children of today and I see problems. I'm not sure they're being taught the proper values. I'm not sure they learn from their experiences."

Reggie did more than just talk, however. Each year he ran a two-day football clinic in his hometown of Chattanooga. He was often accompanied by other top players, such as Ronnie Lott, Jim McMahon, Keith Jackson, and Keith Byars. The players taught the fundamentals of football. But they also talked to the youngsters about life-style, about staying away from drugs, and about the value of education.

"Reggie came right out and said he wanted to give something back to Chattanooga," said Sam Woolwine. "This is just one of the things he does."

Working with his wife Sara, Reggie also headed a weekly support group for the Family Services organization in Philadelphia. He was also active in the Fellowship of Christian Athletes and hosted a weekly radio show in Philly.

Sometimes there seems to be no end to the non-football things that Reggie has done. In 1991 he and his wife Sara built a second home on their 40-acre (16-hectare) tract of land in Maryville, Tennessee. Originally called the Hope Palace and now named the Reggie and Sara White Maternity Home, it was built for the purpose of helping unwed mothers put their lives in order. It was completely funded by the Whites.

As a role model, Reggie has wanted to give all children positive and powerful values. (The Whites have two children: a son Jeremy, born in 1986, and a daughter Jecolia, born in 1988. The name Jecolia means "powerful.") Because he has become a famous athlete, he has tried to do even more. He has said that black professionals should give back with money. They should help create opportunities for the people in the inner cities.

It would be easy for Reggie White to just sit back and enjoy being a famous athlete. He would have plenty of money, and once his career has

Reggie has always taken great pride in his family. Here he poses with his wife Sara, son Jeremy, and daughter Jecolia. Jeremy is ready for a little football.

ended he could live the easy life. But he has always known that there are many things in the world that could be better, and he has decided to help change them. Although he has become a famous athlete, he has never thought of himself as special.

"I walk down the street and people treat me real nice," Reggie has said. "That's what makes me happy. They see I'm real, just like them. There's nothing special about me. They see that I want to be there for them. That's what's important to me."

Then Reggie said something that did make him special. Not many people would have the confidence and courage to say it.

"I'm at peace with myself. I believe in what's right, and I'll stand up for what's right, even if it costs me my life."

REGGIE WHITE: HIGHLIGHTS

1961	Born on December 19 in Chattanooga, Tennessee.
1979	Named high school All-American as defensive tackle at Howard High School in Chattanooga. Also stars for basketball team.
1980	Records 32 tackles, 19 assists, and 2 quarterback sacks as freshman at the University of Tennessee.
1981	Records 61 tackles, 34 assists, and 8 sacks. Named to sophomore All-American team.
1982	Records 36 tackles, 11 assists, and 7 sacks during injury-plagued junior year.
1983	Records 72 tackles, 28 assists, and 15 sacks. Named All-American and Southeastern Conference Player of the Year.
1984	Joins Memphis Showboats of United States Football League. Records 52 solo tackles and 11 sacks. Named to USFL all-rookie team.
1985	Records 68 solo tackles and 12.5 sacks for Memphis. Named to all-USFL first team. Joins Philadelphia Eagles of National Football League (NFL). Named National Football Conference (NFC) Defensive Rookie of the Year. Named to NFL all-rookie first team. Named honorable mention all-pro.
1986	Records 83 unassisted tackles and 18 sacks. Named all-pro. Named Most Valuable Player of Pro Bowl. Son Jeremy born to Reggie and Sara White.
1987	Records 21 sacks in only 12 games. Named all-pro.

1988   Leads NFL in sacks (18) for second straight year.
                Records 133 tackles.
                Named all-pro.
                Daughter Jecolia born to Reggie and Sara White.

1989–1992   Is among NFL leaders in sacks each year.
                Named all-pro each year.

1993   Declares free agency and joins Green Bay Packers. Ties for the NFL lead
                in quarterback sacks with 13.

FIND OUT MORE

Aaseng, Nathan. *Football's Fierce Defenses*. Minneapolis, Minn.: Lerner, 1980.

Balzer, Howard. *Football All Pro Defense*. Fenton, Mo.: Marketcom, 1989.

Football: Superstars & Superstats. Racine, Wisc.: Western Publishing Company, 1991.

Gutman, Bill. *Football*. North Bellmore, N.Y.: Marshall Cavendish, 1990.

Madden, John. *The First Book of Football*. New York: Crown, 1988.

Rambeck, Richard. *Philadelphia Eagles*. Mankato, Minn.: Creative Education, 1991.

Sullivan, George. *All About Football*. New York: Putnam Publishing Group, 1990.

How to write to Reggie White:
Reggie White
c/o Green Bay Packers
1265 Lombardi Avenue
Green Bay, Wisconsin 54307-0628

INDEX